W9-AZD-286

WITHDRAWN

A GRAPHIC HISTORY OF THE CIVIL RIGHTS MOVEMENT

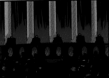

THURGOOD MARSHALL:
THE SUPREME COURT RULES ON "SEPARATE BUT EQUAL"

BY GARY JEFFREY
ILLUSTRATED BY JOHN AGGS

Gareth Stevens
Publishing

Please visit our website, www.garethstevens.com.
For a free color catalog of all our high-quality books,
call toll free 1-800-542-2595 or fax 1-877-542-2596.

Library of Congress Cataloging-in-Publication Data

Jeffrey, Gary.
Thurgood Marshall : the Supreme Court rules on "separate but equal" /
Gary Jeffrey.
p. cm. — (Graphic History of the Civil Rights Movement)
Includes index.
ISBN 978-1-4339-7504-2 (pbk.)
ISBN 978-1-4339-7505-9 (6-pack)
ISBN 978-1-4339-7503-5 (library binding)
1. African Americans—Civil rights—History. 2. Civil rights movements—
United States—History. 3. Equality before the law—United States. 4. Civil
rights—United States. 5. United States. Supreme Court. 6. Marshall,
Thurgood, 1908-1993. I. Title.
KF4757.J44 2012
342.7308'73—dc23
2011045579

J-GN
B
MARSHALL
412-8859

First Edition

Published in 2013 by
Gareth Stevens Publishing
111 East 14th Street, Suite 349
New York, NY 10003

Designed by David West Books

Printed in China

CPSIA compliance information: Batch #DWS12GS: For further information contact Gareth Stevens, New York, New York at 1-800-542-2595.

CONTENTS

The trouble began with Lincoln's assassination on April 14, 1865. Andrew Johnson, the vice president, was sworn in and, while Congress was away over the summer, issued pardons to Southern war leaders who swore allegiance. In December 1865, the 13th Amendment abolishing slavery was passed, but the Southern leadership made it clear they had no intention of accepting their former slaves as equals.

President Johnson wanted to let the South settle the freed slaves back into society in their own way.

CIVIL RIGHTS

So called "black codes" restricting former slaves' rights began appearing in the South. Freedmen and Republicans in the North got angry—it was as if the war had never happened! They drafted the 14th Amendment

Freedmen gather to vote in New Orleans in 1867.

protecting black citizenship and constitutional rights. The 15th Amendment of 1870 guaranteed the right to vote, and for the first time, African Americans took some part in running their country.

This progress came at a cost—the federal government had to occupy the South with troops to force the changes through—a period known as Reconstruction.

In the reconstructed South, black Mississippians like John Roy Lynch successfully ran for Congress.

CIVIL WRONGS

During Reconstruction, the white supremacists of the South used violence and scare tactics to stop blacks from getting education and voting. Although the government took action against groups like the Ku Klux Klan, they were more focused on building the economy. To the dismay of Northern reformers, the South was reverting to type as African Americans saw their civil rights being taken away again.

The Ku Klux Klan formed the terror arm of white opposition to black progress in the South.

SEPARATING ACTS

Federal troops left the South in 1877, ending Reconstruction. As a last gasp at protecting blacks against discrimination, the Republicans had passed the Civil Rights Act of 1875. In 1883, it got ruled unconstitutional, leaving the way open for Southern legislatures to bring in their own rules separating the white and black races in public—segregation.

Black leaders were incensed. They felt they had been sold out and began to get organized to fight these new threats to their freedom in any way they could...

The new restrictions were like the black codes under another name, "Jim Crow" laws, named after a black minstrel figure, an object of ridicule to Southern whites.

5

Thurgood Marshall: The Supreme Court Rules on "Separate but Equal"

THE STORY OF "SEPARATE BUT EQUAL" BEGAN IN THE FIRST-CLASS WHITES-ONLY COMPARTMENT OF A TRAIN BOUND FOR NEW ORLEANS, LOUISIANA, ON JUNE 7, 1892...

...AND YOU REALIZE OF COURSE, GENTLEMEN, THAT I AM **BLACK**.

HOMER PLESSY WAS A **PLANT**. HE HAD BEEN CHOSEN BY THE CITIZENS COMMITTEE TO CHALLENGE THE RECENTLY PASSED SEPARATE CAR LAW.

THE CREATIVE SOCIAL ENGINEER SHOULD BE ABLE TO USE THE **CONSTITUTION** TO FORCE THROUGH CHANGES THAT COULD *NEVER* HAPPEN IN **POLITICS.**

THE MESSAGE WAS NOT LOST ON MARSHALL.

ON NOVEMBER 5, 1935, AS A LAWYER FOR THE NATIONAL ASSOCIATION FOR THE ADVANCEMENT OF COLORED PEOPLE, HE GOT TO *ACT* ON IT.

...SINCE THE STATE OF MARYLAND HAS **NOT** PROVIDED A BLACK LAW SCHOOL ON THE SAME LEVEL, MY CLIENT, DONALD MURRAY, **SHOULD** BE ALLOWED TO ATTEND THE WHITE UNIVERSITY.

MURRAY HAD BEEN DENIED ENTRY BY THE SAME LAW SCHOOL THAT HAD REFUSED MARSHALL.

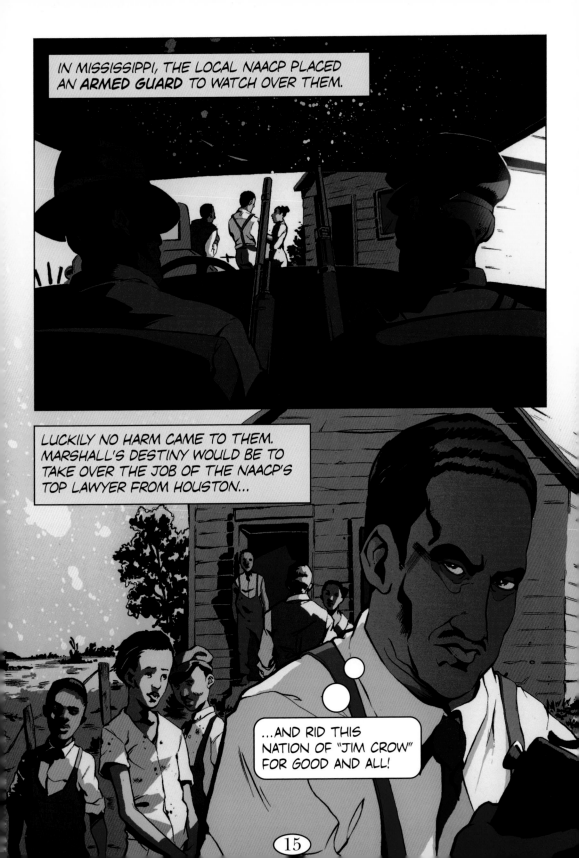

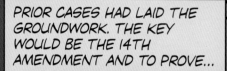

BY THE LATE 1940S, MARSHALL AND HIS TEAM OF LAWYERS AT THE NAACP HAD HELPED AFRICAN AMERICANS BATTLE FOR VOTING RIGHTS, HOUSING, AND GRADUATE EDUCATION, BUT MARSHALL HAD HIS EYE ON A **BIGGER PRIZE**...

...THE PLESSY DECISION. IT'S STOOD FOR NEARLY SIXTY YEARS. NOW IS OUR CHANCE **TO TAKE IT DOWN.**

FOREVER!

PRIOR CASES HAD LAID THE GROUNDWORK. THE KEY WOULD BE THE 14TH AMENDMENT AND TO PROVE...

...THAT SEGREGATED SCHOOLS ARE **HARMFUL** TO OUR BLACK CHILDREN!

BEGINNING IN SEPTEMBER 1951, A NUMBER OF BLACK PARENTS WERE ASKED TO ATTEMPT TO ENROLL THEIR CHILDREN IN WHITE-ONLY PUBLIC SCHOOLS IN ORDER TO GET REJECTION LETTERS THAT COULD START THE **LEGAL CHALLENGE.**

In 1955, the Supreme Court received arguments from white-only schools asking for money to enable them to change. The court ordered them to desegregate "with all deliberate speed." Some southern schools took this as an excuse to leave things just the way they were.

No Turning Back

Having defeated school segregation, civil rights activists next turned their attention to Jim Crow on public transport and in restaurants. *Brown v. Board of Education* had started a civil rights struggle that would rage for the next ten years.

In 1957, the state governor used troops to block the integration of Little Rock Central High School in Arkansas.

A Supreme Career

Brown v. Board of Education had also thrust Thurgood Marshall into the spotlight. President Kennedy appointed him to the United States Court of Appeals in 1961. President Lyndon B. Johnson made him United States Solicitor General in 1965. Two years later, he became an associate justice on the Supreme Court—a position he held for the next 24 years.

Thurgood Marshall firmly believed the law was the best route toward equality.

GLOSSARY

abolishing Ending, eliminating.

activists People who fight to make a change to improve society.

allegiance Loyalty.

amendment A change or addition made to the Constitution.

assassination The murder of a leader or a person in power.

inferiority The condition of being less or worse than someone or something else.

pardon Forgiveness granted by the government for a crime.

pioneered Invented, was the first to develop.

plaintiff The person who accuses another of a crime in a court of law.

psychological Related to the mind.

reverting Going back to a previous idea or way of thinking.

ruse A plot or trick intended to deceive someone.

segregation The separation of blacks and whites in public.

supremacists Those who believe that one group of people is better than, or superior to, another group.

INDEX